MW00668263

Also by Jonathan J. Clark

WORKING BACKWARDS

Eight Steps to Performance Improvement and Operational Excellence For All Organizations

BROWN BEAR PUBLISHING

THE STORY OF KODIAK CAKES

Ten Lessons
for Starting Your Own Business

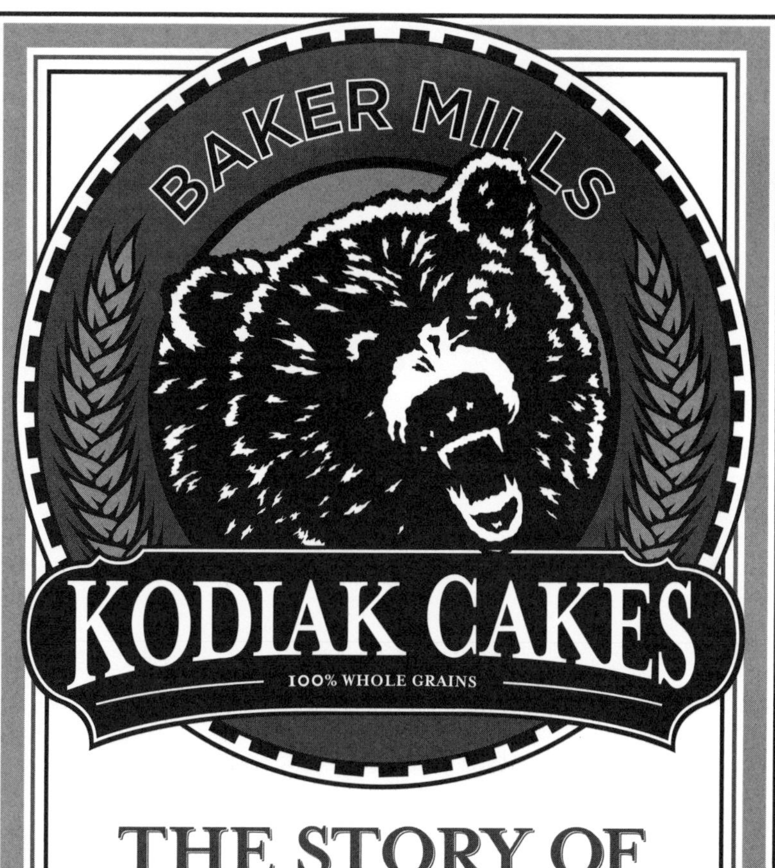

THE STORY OF KODIAK CAKES

TEN LESSONS FOR STARTING YOUR OWN BUSINESS

JONATHAN J. CLARK

Library of Congress Control Number: 2009904934

ISBN-10: 0982491808

ISBN-13: 978-0-9824918-0-5

BUSINESS & MANAGEMENT/Entrepreneurship
BISAC: BUS025000

Published by Brown Bear Publishing
P.O. Box 521938, Salt Lake City, Utah 84152-1938

Edited by Elizabeth Hokanson

www.kodiakcakes.com

Book design and layout by Todd Schofield

Printed in the United States of America

To Mom, Grandpa, Great-Grandpa,
and the American dream

TABLE OF CONTENTS

Without Mom, there would be no Baker Mills or its first product, Kodiak Cakes Frontier Flapjack & Waffle Mix, to write about. Mom was the one who suggested and inspired me to start the company in the first place. Without Grandpa there would be no Kodiak Cakes either, since Kodiak Cakes was based upon the hotcakes he cooked for his family while Mom grew up. And without Great-Grandpa, Peter Julius Christofeson, who was born in 1843 in Denmark and immigrated to the United States, there would be no American dream to pursue. Because of these three marvelous people, Kodiak Cakes became a reality. However, like most successes, Baker Mills and its products did not come from the merits of just one person or even a few, but from the contributions of many people. I also wish to thank them.

Kodiak Cakes would not be the product it is without the superb expertise and creativity of graphic artist Todd Schofield, who designed the Kodiak Cakes logo and packaging. My younger brother, Joel Clark, has been president of Baker Mills for over a decade, growing it into a most successful company. My dad, Richard Clark, also devoted many years to expanding the company as he worked alongside Joel to promote Kodiak Cakes and place the product in stores across the country. My older brother, Tim Clark, helped name Kodiak Cakes, wrote the story on the back of the package, and helped position the product. Our great friend, Gary Buehner, invested $13,000 in Baker Mills so that Joel and I could take Kodiak Cakes to the next level. Years later, Gary let us buy back his portion of the company for the same $13,000 without interest, just because he wanted to see us succeed. Finally, though I have not the space to name them all, many other family members, friends, suppliers, vendors, distributors, and ultimately our faithful customers have contributed much in making Kodiak Cakes what it is today.

INTRODUCTION

From the time I was eight years old, I wanted to go into business as my life's profession. In fact, my dream was to start my own company. At the time I didn't realize that for many, that dream was known as "the American dream." I learned that later in life while setting out to fulfill it.

I'm not in the league of billionaire entrepreneurs who have started numerous massive and phenomenally successful organizations. I'm just a common business founder, perhaps like you, who wanted to start a company that would succeed. I trained for this career in college. I also read books about the process of starting a business. I interviewed many successful entrepreneurs to learn what worked for them, and I worked for other organizations to gain experience. Finally, I set out to accomplish my dream. It was exciting, motivating, and grueling. But with the help of many extraordinary people, Baker Mills and its first product, Kodiak Cakes Frontier Flapjack & Waffle Mix, became tremendously successful.

Unfortunately many companies and products don't succeed. In business school I was repeatedly taught that only one in ten businesses succeeds and that only one in ten products succeeds. Through the years I have regularly witnessed this low success rate as numerous companies opened their doors with great hopes but eventually went under, while their newly launched products disappeared. Why is this? Some highly successful entrepreneurs I have interviewed humbly attribute their success to just plain luck. Does this mean that others were just unlucky? Well, I'm not sure I fully believe in luck. Perhaps luck is a factor in some instances, but overall I believe successful entrepreneurs have more than luck on their sides—they follow sound business principles that aid them in their success and minimize their risk.

Maybe we had some luck with Kodiak Cakes, which gave us a taste of the American dream. But I like to think that we tried to apply the knowledge we learned from seasoned professionals and through our own personal experiences. These experiences and the desire to help others reduce the high casualty rate of new businesses motivated me to write this book. I wanted to tell the story of Kodiak Cakes, because it's a great a story, but I also wanted to share the valuable lessons we discovered in our venture. Many of these lessons came through trial and error as we set out to compete in a mature market where legendary industry giants were ever prevalent. I am confident that this story and these ten lessons will help you in your venture to realize the American dream.

"Simply put … the best pancakes I have ever eaten."

—Salt Lake City, Utah

KODIAK CAKES: THE STORY

The story of Kodiak Cakes and the prospect of pursuing the American dream really started with my great-grandfather, Peter Julius Christofferson. He was born in Denmark in 1843. Peter was a fearless man, and typical of many Danes, was unusually strong. As a young man he immigrated to the United States and eventually moved to Lehi, Utah, a small farming town south of Salt Lake City. In fact, the 1984 movie *Footloose*, starring Kevin Bacon, was filmed in Lehi.

A family story tells of a man in Lehi who had purchased two hundred-pound sacks of flour and needed help carrying them across the street. Peter offered to carry both sacks at the same time. The man responded, "You couldn't do that." Peter replied, "I can carry them and you too." So with the man on one shoulder and 200 pounds of flour on the other, my grandfather crossed the street. As little children, we thought that was pretty heroic.

Another story recounts that Peter was involved in the Black Hawk Indian War for three years (1865 - 1867). During this time he was once crossing a river on horseback alone when Indian warriors on the opposite bank spotted him and were ready to shoot him with their arrows. But Chief Black Hawk forbade them because of his respect for Peter's bravery.

One of Peter's many children was my grandfather, Wallace Christofferson, who was born in 1902 in Lehi. He was also a good man, known for his courage and strength. When Grandpa was two years old, his mother died, and when he was eight his father, Peter, died. Grandpa was passed around to his older siblings, who looked after him. While living with them he worked at the town flour mill, Lehi Roller Mills, featured in *Footloose*, which after a hundred years is still processing and distributing flour and grain. In fact, all these years later, Kodiak Cakes is produced using whole-wheat flour purchased from Lehi Roller Mills.

Grandpa's growing up years were rather rough. So in 1917, while the First World War was raging, Grandpa left Lehi to join the United States Marines. In order to enlist he stated his age as eighteen, though he was only fifteen. The Marines provided good opportunities for Grandpa: military training, education, and sports. Grandpa loved football and became a member of one of the Marines football teams. Although he enjoyed playing football, he also had another passion: boxing. Years later he would spar with the grandkids in a friendly way, trying to trick us with a touch to the head, followed by a quick, unsuspected soft jab to the stomach. I still remember his big smile as he gently fooled us with his quick hands.

Grandpa told us that after the war he fought the great world heavyweight boxer Jack Dempsey in a prizefight held in Lehi. Dempsey was in Utah and traveled from town to town challenging the toughest man in each one. Grandpa told us that right after the fight started, he connected with a solid punch and hit Dempsey a good one in the jaw. But after that Dempsey got the best of Grandpa and cut him below the eye, giving him a scar he proudly displayed the rest of his life.

Grandpa later married my grandmother, Ada Baker, who was born in 1900. Her mother, Sarah Mills, was born in 1868. My mom receives credit for naming the company I would later start, Baker Mills, the maiden names of her mother and grandmother—a perfect name for a whole grain food manufacturing company. After Grandpa and Grandma married, an incident occurred while they were living in Los Angeles that typified Grandpa's strength and character. While walking down a dark street, Grandma and Grandpa saw two men trying to molest a lady. Grandpa ran over, threw the men off the woman, grabbed both men—one in each arm—and hauled them off.

After about fifteen years of marriage, Grandpa was called on a mission for his church in the Northeast United States, leaving his wife and four children for nearly two years. This was during the Korean War, and times were hard. Typically, younger men were called into missionary service, but since young men were being drafted to war, some of the older men were called on missions in their stead. Grandma struggled to sustain Grandpa as a missionary and provide for the family.

When Grandpa came home from his mission, he returned to work with the Southern Pacific Railroad, where he was an engineer. Later in life he lost much of his hearing due to spending so many years driving the loud trains. As grandchildren we learned to shout to communicate with Grandpa.

Grandpa was truly a great man with a gentle demeanor. I still remember him calling Grandma "Mommy Dear." One Sunday evening, when my mom, Penny, was sixteen years old, she and Grandpa were walking home from church. Grandpa, being a gentleman, stepped around her to the outside as they crossed a street when suddenly a car came speeding straight toward them. Grandpa took the terrible impact, savings Mom's life. However, the car crushed Grandpa's leg and put Mom in the hospital. In time Mom recovered, but Grandpa's leg was permanently damaged, so he was never again the fine athlete he had been.

As Mom grew up in northern Utah, Grandpa regularly cooked up hearty hotcakes for breakfast. Grandpa's great-tasting hotcakes were made from whole wheat that he hand-ground into flour. These hotcakes were thick and fluffy, made by whipping up egg whites and folding them into a bubbly batter. The bubbles were a result of adding baking soda and vinegar to the batter, an old-fashioned way to make it fluffier.

Fortunately, after Mom got married she kept Grandpa's hotcakes tradition alive, nothing varying from his old-fashioned recipe. Waking up to the familiar aroma of hotcakes in the morning was a comfortable way to ease out of a deep sleep. Then one summer day in 1982, Mom decided she would mix up the dry ingredients of Grandpa's recipe and have Joel, our eight-year-old brother, sell them around the neighborhood in brown paper lunch sacks. She had thought about the idea for months and believed there was a market for good-tasting, easy-to-make whole grain mixes.

As Mom got ready to make the mixes, she realized she didn't have enough money to buy all the dry ingredients that were required. I remember walking into our kitchen at age sixteen and hearing Mom talking to her mother on the phone. I heard her ask her for fifty dollars to buy a fifty-pound sack of nonfat dry milk, which she needed to make the pancake mix. Initially Grandma wasn't sure she wanted to give Mom the money, thinking her idea may not work. But a few days later Grandma consented and gave her the fifty dollars to start her company.

After obtaining the money, Mom purchased everything she needed for her mix. I remember walking into our kitchen and seeing the counter covered with opened brown paper lunch bags. On the outside of each sack were the mixing and cooking instructions that Mom had carefully handwritten. She had the most beautiful handwriting. Mom filled each sack with carefully measured dry ingredients, consisting of whole-wheat flour, nonfat dry milk, salt, and baking soda. She had ground the wheat herself in our electric grinder. After each bag was filled, she gently folded down the tops of each one and gave them to

Joel, who placed the pancake mixes into his red Radio Flyer wagon. Once he was loaded up, he was off to sell them through the neighborhood with our Old English sheepdog, Moe. Mom thought this would be a good thing for Joel to do to keep him busy. Joel happily walked up to the front doors of homes in our neighborhood to sell the mixes. He sold all the mixes and returned home for more.

Although the neighbors requested more of her delicious mix, Mom's enterprise was short-lived because she was busy raising her five children. However, she learned what she had hoped for—that most people were delighted with a healthy whole-grain mix. Over the next twelve years, the thoughts of her father's hotcakes never left her mind. Finally, in the summer of 1994 it was time once again to fulfill her business dream. So Mom urged me, one of her three sons, to formally start a company that made a high-end, delicious whole grain pancake mix resembling Grandpa's hotcakes. She thought I could fill this niche and later add other whole grain mixes. She said, "Jon, I even have a name for your company—Baker Mills."

BAKER MILLS

In 1994 I began my venture with Baker Mills. My challenge was to modify Grandpa's recipe into a delicious and nourishing "add water only" mix. My first task was to purchase dry ingredients so I could start experimenting. I went to a local grain and flour distributor where I could buy a fifty-pound bag of whole-wheat flour. When I arrived I asked a man out on the dock for a bag of whole-wheat flour. To my surprise he asked me what kind of wheat I wanted. I told him again, "Whole wheat." To my dismay, he told me there were different kinds of wheat. He asked if I wanted red wheat, white wheat, soft or hard, spring or winter. I didn't know. I told him I would get back to him and decided I needed to go to the library to figure out this question.

So I went to the Salt Lake County Library and spent a lot of time reading. Not only did I research wheat, but I read through a bunch of cookbooks to see what ingredients other pancake and waffle mix recipes included. Some recipes used corn, rice, barley, oats, millet, and other grains. As a result I ended up researching every kind of grain I could think of. I learned about how easy or hard they were to digest, their nutritional qualities, storage aspects, taste, and cooking performance. When I was done with my library research, I purchased many pancake and waffle mixes from grocery and specialty stores to analyze their ingredients and taste each one.

To add to my research, I talked to grain mills, food experts, and food companies from places all around the country to identify what other dry ingredients I should experiment with. I found these company names at the University of Utah library, since the Internet wasn't fully functioning back then. However, the more I learned, the more complicated matters became. Grain mills asked me if I wanted to change the water content in the wheat flour, how finely I wanted the grain milled, and if I wanted to keep the germ in the "whole wheat." One milling company told me that some products used the term "whole wheat" on their ingredient list but didn't include the germ of the wheat. This was because keeping the germ in the flour shortens the shelf life to one year. I never found out if that was actually true, but knew I would keep the wheat germ in my flour since it is so healthy. I was told to be sure to state "100 percent whole wheat" on my ingredient list. In addition, one food expert asked me how I would subdue or offset the natural acidic flavor of the whole wheat that so many children don't care for. I had no idea.

As I looked into other dry ingredients, I realized there was more to learn. For example, dried sweeteners included several kinds of dried honeys, dried molasses, raw sugars, and refined sugars, to name a few. Dried milk products were mostly composed of low-heat, medium-heat, and high-heat powdered milk, nonfat milk, sweat cream buttermilk, and whey. Dried eggs just smelled bad, but then I learned that dried egg whites smelled much better, didn't contain fat, and lasted longer. However, they were by far the most expensive ingredient I would end up using. Even just plain salt had to be carefully thought through, since I could buy sea salt, natural salt containing some brownish -looking minerals, iodized salt, or non-iodized.

Baking powder was also more complex than I had ever imagined. Should I use a baking powder that was premade, like the kind you can buy in the store, or would I need to develop my own formula? I learned that baking powder could be made from a variety of FDA-approved food-grade chemicals. I later used ordinary baking powder ingredients.

After all this research, I went to a dry ingredient food show. I couldn't believe all the different products that were available. Besides cinnamon, I realized I could get nearly any flavor or food item I wanted in a powdered form, such as dried vanilla flavoring, dried blueberries, or powered raspberry flavoring.

Finally I obtained samples of all the different kinds of dry ingredients I thought I should experiment with to formulate a delicious "add water only" recipe. My kitchen looked like a chemistry lab, with bags and containers of various shapes and sizes on the table, counters, and floor. It took some time before I realized that I actually needed to weigh the ingredients in order to be consistent with each batch, rather than using measuring cups and spoons.

After some research I purchased a certified gram scale. It cost $400. This really turned my kitchen into a food lab, as I was now carefully weighing each ingredient and recording how much I used. I had pages of notes all over and tons of plastic bags full of the different mixes I had created using slightly different ingredients. Since I was working full time at another company, I had to experiment on evenings and weekends. I tested batch after batch with my wife and then let family and friends sample the best ones.

It was interesting to learn that incorrect amounts of some ingredients could cause the pancakes to burn on the outside.

Other ingredients caused the pancakes to be truly distasteful or fall apart after they were cooked. Still others gave the pancakes a strange texture, color, or aftertaste, while some ingredients prevented the batter from easily mixing. Some ingredients made the pancakes too moist on the inside after they were cooked.

To avoid putting oil in the mix, or to prevent having to add oil to the batter when making waffles, I discovered I just needed to use more of the expensive dry egg whites and nonfat dry milk. I also learned that if I used enough dry honey I could counter the acidic wheat flavor. In fact, I remember talking to a food science expert in California about my recipe, trying to get some tips. He asked me what percent of the mix was egg whites and dry milk. After I told him, he said, "Your product will never make it. Your ingredients are too expensive, and customers won't spend that much on a pancake mix." I decided not to pay any attention to him and continued developing the best pancake mix I could. I wasn't interested in making a cheaper pancake in order to increase my profit. I felt profit would come on its own if I produced a high-quality product.

After several months of testing batch after batch and sampling the mixes with other people, I felt confident I had achieved the perfect mix in terms of flavor, color, texture, and performance. However, I still couldn't get one thing right—the baking powder. This was by far the most difficult part. My challenge was to produce a pancake mix made with heavier whole grains that actually cooked up light and fluffy. I wasn't sure how I could get the pancakes to be as light and fluffy as Grandpa's.

Finally I got in touch with a chemist at a large company that produced the ingredients for popular brands of baking powder in grocery stores. He explained everything I needed to know about baking powder and helped me develop a formula that made the pancakes perfectly light and fluffy. The formula was so good that I realized I could even use Belgian waffle irons to make waffles with the mix, since they came out so thick. It was sensational!

The chemist taught me that baking powder is just like adding baking soda to vinegar, as Grandpa had done. Baking soda, as we learn in chemistry class, is a base, and vinegar is an acid. When the two combine, they sizzle and emit carbon dioxide or bubbles. The great thing about wheat is that it contains gluten, which sticks together when it is in a dough form. The bubbles then get trapped in the gluten, which causes the dough to rise and become fluffy.

The chemist told me that instead of using a liquid acid, like vinegar, we could replace it with a dry food-grade chemical that would produce the same bubbly result when combined with water. This produces what is known as a "single-acting" baking powder. As soon as water is added to a mix containing the two chemicals, bubbles start forming. If we were to add another dry food-grade chemical to the baking soda, it would produce even more bubbles when exposed to heat. This would produce what is known as "double-acting" baking powder. As soon as the pancake batter containing all three chemicals was poured on the hot griddle, the pancakes would rise even more.

The dilemma we faced was combining the right amounts of each chemical so they would cancel each other out in the bubbling process and thereby eliminate any baking powder aftertaste. Since some ingredients in the mix already contained some acid, such as eggs and milk, we had to account for that amount of acid as well and adjust the baking powder formula accordingly. After more experimentation, we finally got the proportions right, and the final "add water only" recipe was done!

The recipe was indeed much more expensive to make than so many competitive products, since it contained natural and wholesome ingredients. However, through the process I learned that achieving taste, nutrition, and convenience all in one product costs a premium. On the other hand, attaining just good taste is easy and cheap. Bleached white flour, sugar, and shortening, relatively inexpensive ingredients, can provide good taste, but they lack nutritional value. Achieving taste and nutrition using whole foods costs a lot more, since honey, whole grains, nonfat dry milk, and nonfat egg whites are much more expensive. Ultimately, achieving taste, nutrition, and convenience—the three pillars of an outstanding food product—costs the most, since they require large proportions of the best ingredients available.

In the end, my "add water only" pancake and waffle mix consisted of 100 percent whole wheat flour, 100 percent whole oat flour, nonfat dry milk, dry honey (consisting of honey and a small amount of starch, which acts as a carrying agent during the drying process), baking powder, dry egg whites, and salt. Once made up, the pancakes were thick, fluffy, natural, and delicious. The mix would not only taste great, but it would be healthy and easy to make.

KODIAK CAKES

One evening, sometime before I finalized the recipe, I went to my brother Tim's house to test a batch of the pancakes. I served them to his family for dinner, and they loved them. Afterward we talked about the pancake mix and explored marketing ideas for the product. I had told Tim that the mix included whole wheat and oat flour, similar to the flapjacks old-timers made back in the days of the North American frontier. I had read this during my research at the library. As we talked, Tim suggested that we give the mix a powerful name that brought people back to nature and the frontier. He had some phenomenal ideas, and we finally decided on Kodiak Cakes Frontier Flapjack & Waffle Mix, named after the massive Kodiak bear indigenous to Kodiak Island, Alaska.

Another reason for choosing the name Kodiak Cakes was that I had been to Alaska on a big fishing trip and always dreamed of going back one day to Kodiak Island. I thought if I named the product Kodiak Cakes I could take a sales trip to the island and deduct it as a business expense. However, fifteen years later, I still hope to make that trip.

Tim also came up with clever ideas for the look and feel of the packaging and even wrote a story for the back of the package. I think it's amazing:

KODIAK CAKES® – RESTORING THE FLAPJACK TRADITION

Years ago, flapjacks were the hearty mainstay of frontiersmen from the frigid Yukon to the wilds of Alaska, and from the Rocky Mountains to the high Sierras. These rugged mountain men and homesteaders relied on a traditional flapjack that combined the rich, substantial taste of whole grain wheat with the light mellow taste of whole grain oats. Although the old-timers knew of the excellent taste and abundant energy they received from their daily tradition, they didn't fully realize that they had stumbled onto a superb nutritional combination. Their flapjacks contained a powerful source of carbohydrates, protein, and fiber—all with very little fat. Since then, the original flapjack has quietly disappeared from North American tables. Today, few people even know that the frontier flapjack and the ordinary pancake are not the same. Many are now discovering for the first time that the original flapjack tastes a

> whole lot better than the lifeless creations that commonly pass for pan-cakes these days. At Baker Mills®, we set out to restore the flapjack tradition. In the process, we soon realized we had to get serious about ingredients—*real taste and real nutrition demand real ingredients*.® The old recipe could not be compromised for profit. Inexpensive fillers such as bleached flour, white sugar, vegetable shortening, and artificial additives that have taken over so many baking products were definitely out of the question. Only with a commitment to using the original ingredients could we restore this lost tradition. We believe we have made good on our commitment with Kodiak Cakes,® using only the finest American wheat and Canadian oats. Kodiak Cakes® are not for the fainthearted, but for those who, like the old frontiersmen, exploring and settling untamed wildernesses, require nutrition, vitality, and taste.

Before we settled on a product name and direction for the packaging, I attended my ten-year high school reunion in the summer of 1994. This is where my luck really ran deep. While I was waiting in the banquet line, my old neighborhood friend since the fifth grade, Todd Schofield, was standing right in front of me. It was great to see him again! Since I hadn't seen him for several years, I asked him what he was doing for work. He told me he was a graphic artist. When he told me this, my eyes opened wide. I was in need of a graphic artist. I remembered an experience in elementary school when Todd had written my name in the fanciest block letters I had ever seen. I knew from that experience that he was a gifted artist. It made sense that he had gone into that profession. I told him about the pancake mix company I was starting and asked if he would design a logo and do the packaging design for me. He was excited to help, and within a few weeks we met for the first time to discuss the vision of going back to the old North American frontier on the Kodiak Cakes package design.

Todd had phenomenal ideas and was even more talented than I suspected. We met over the course of many months as he developed the perfect logo and packaging design. Since we both had day jobs, we often met in his basement apartment well into the nights, where he had a home office he used for freelance work. We were often at grocery stores at midnight studying the design of competitive products and measuring the dimensions of their packaging.

As Todd worked on the Kodiak Cakes design, his objective was to get consumers "back to the basics," as he liked to say, using a simple but classic and rugged design. The amount of time Todd devoted to the logo and packaging design, the master carton design, our sales brochure, photographing layouts for our Web site, developing additional product designs, and helping me with so many other details was staggering. We were excited as we worked together on Kodiak Cakes and had high hopes for the product taking off in the market. Todd even purchased a new computer for $8,000 on his limited budget so he could use updated software and have the processing speed and memory required for the design.

While he was focused on the design, I learned about bar coding, trademarks, and nutrition facts while finding suppliers and negotiating pricing. Since I didn't have much money, I had to do most of this work myself rather than outsourcing it. I went to the University of Utah library to look up trademarks and contacted the United States Patent and Trademark Office for information on how to submit a trademark. I later had to hire an attorney, who gave me a discount, to complete the trademarking process.

I also met with the Food and Drug Administration to get manuals on nutrition facts and regulations. In addition I obtained bar coding manuals and figured out how to get a UPC (Universal Product Code) number on the package. It took a lot of work, and I still can't believe I read through so much information and talked to so many experts. But eventually everything started coming together.

After Todd had completed a number of iterations of the logo and package design, we finally thought his design had reached perfection. He spent much additional time getting the colors just right by experimenting with a printing company to ensure we had picked out the correct packaging paper. We started with a two-and-a-half-pound bag but later migrated to a twenty-four

-ounce box. We then turned our attention to developing the master carton—the corrugated box that would hold twelve bags of Kodiak Cakes. We had to determine the weight of the cardboard we needed to see how many boxes we could stack on a pallet before the bottom cases would collapse from the jarring of a long-distance transport in a semi truck.

As we put the finishing touches on the product, I tried to figure out how to best manufacture it. I looked at every possible avenue—from producing it myself to outsourcing the production to other companies. I researched mixing and boxing machinery as well as warehousing space and labor costs. I put together pro forma financial statements that projected what volumes I needed to sell in order to break even under different scenarios. Since I didn't have much money, I had to figure out how I would get financing. This became an increasing concern for me as I continued to move forward with my venture.

I had bought and sold a pickup truck, which gave me $1,400 profit to spend on the company. However, little did I realize I would need much more. As financial needs increased, I refinanced my family car, applied for credit cards, used our checking account cash reserve, took out my meager retirement and paid the early withdrawal penalty, and allocated as much money as my wife and I could afford. It was extremely challenging! We lived on little. Every dollar mattered. I remember once thinking that I really needed ten dollars for groceries. Eventually I was able to come up with about $23,500 to start the company. My dad and my brother Tim, seeing my need for more money, gave me $1,100 and $650, respectively, which helped tremendously. The total bill for starting the company was about $25,000.

However, since I didn't want to give up any ownership of the company to an equity investor, I initially refused to seek money outside the family. In addition, since I had no capital assets other than our family car and an old pickup truck, I couldn't get a bank loan. But I don't think I would have preferred a loan anyway. Growing up, I was taught to avoid borrowing money as much as possible. Using credit cards with low limits, taking money from my checking account cash reserve at the bank, and refinancing our car was as much as I was willing to borrow. In addition, I had worked for a wonderfully successful manufacturing firm that had no debt. This was the founder's philosophy, which had greatly influenced me. So we scraped to get by over the next few years.

In retrospect, having so little money was actually a great blessing. It forced me to learn everything about the business and to do much of the work myself rather than outsourcing it. Having invested so much personal time and sacrifice in the company also made me feel more empowered to compete with competitors, more assertive in negotiating pricing with suppliers, and more confident in pursuing sales with customers.

With my limit of capital, I concluded that the best and most economical method for producing Kodiak Cakes would be to outsource the manufacturing. After more research I found a company that would blend and package the ingredients if I delivered the raw materials to them and picked up the finished product. To accommodate this plan, I cleaned out my nearly empty and unfinished walk-out basement. I scrubbed the cement floors and sectioned off an area for the raw ingredients and finished product. I had to build a platform using two-by-four -inch boards and four-by-eight-foot sheets of plywood so the product could be off the ground to meet code. (I had checked with the state to make sure I met their requirements.) The storage area was sealed off with long sheets of plastic hanging from the basement ceiling. Outside this inventory room was my old desk, a basic phone with a cassette tape answering machine, my school computer, and a new thermal paper fax machine. It was all makeshift, but it was the best I could do in the duplex we were renting under the circumstances.

After I ordered the necessary raw ingredients, packaging, and master cartons, trucks started to show up at our duplex, including a huge eighteen-wheeler semi truck. Other than occasional moving vans in the neighborhood, I imagine this eighteen-wheeler was the biggest truck to ever drive on our street. I think the driver was hoping to back his truck up to a dock and remove the pallets with a forklift. But he was a good sport and helped my brother Joel and me carry the freshly printed Kodiak Cakes paper bags and cardboard master cartons into my garage. It took a long time to get the 25,000 printed bags and 2,500 boxes off the truck. They filled my entire one-car garage. When the raw ingredients arrived, I stored them in my basement.

After I received all the raw materials, I loaded up my old red and white 1978 Ford pickup truck with enough product to make the first batch of Kodiak Cakes. It was a cold, snowy day, and the roads were bad, so I put chains on my truck to drive on the icy roads to the manufacturing facility. I delivered all the materials, and a couple weeks later I was back to pick up my first batch of finished Kodiak Cakes. After a year and a half of so much tremendous effort, Kodiak Cakes Frontier Flapjack & Waffle Mix was ready for market. It was the end of November 1995.

Just two months before I picked up my first batch of Kodiak Cakes, my brother Joel returned from a two-year church mission in Australia. He arrived at precisely the right time to help me sell and market the product. It had been thirteen years since Joel had sold Mom's mixes in the neighborhood, pulling his wagon down the streets.

Joel was now a young man, but he still had his delightful, optimistic personality. And with it he began selling Kodiak Cakes to gift, specialty, and sporting good stores in Salt Lake City and the surrounding area. After some good success, Joel and I decided to expand our sales market outside the state of Utah. Our first sales trip was to Jackson Hole, Wyoming. During the early winter in December 1995, we loaded up my car and left at 4 AM to drive up to Jackson Hole. We drove all morning and arrived in Jackson Hole about five hours later, not long before the gift shops opened. We divided the town in half and went to work selling Kodiak Cakes to the gift stores. We talked to store owners and managers about our product and gave many away so they could take them home and try them. We felt successful, as many stores bought a case of Kodiak Cakes. At about 5 PM we left for home, having sold all nineteen cases that we could fit in our car.

We soon ventured off on another long, one-day sales trip to Sun Valley, Idaho. Then we sold Kodiak Cakes to gift shops in other resort areas such as Park City, Sundance, Midway, and Snowbird, Utah. Selling our product was actually quite fun. People responded to it in such a positive, enthusiastic way, purchasing more than I anticipated. We also gave away many bags to help spread the word and gain a small customer following.

What made our marketing efforts really satisfying were the enthusiastic letters we started receiving from our customers who had purchased Kodiak Cakes while on vacation in the resort towns we had visited. Customers told us how much they loved the product and asked where they could buy it locally. We were thrilled to read these letters. One huge multibillion-dollar food manufacturing company that expressed interest in buying Kodiak Cakes told me that a single letter represented 1,000 happy customers. We weren't anywhere near having that many customers. Joel and I were astonished.

Based on the positive customer responses we decided to begin selling Kodiak Cakes to local grocery stores. We were excited when the grocery store buyers we met with told us they would like to carry our product. As part of our sales calls, we often cooked up samples of Kodiak Cakes right there in their corporate offices. From this we learned that the formal term for sampling the product was called a "cutting." In fact, we were entirely unfamiliar with the grocery industry jargon, purchasing protocol, markups, and acronyms. So we had to naively ask the grocery store buyers to help us through the process when they asked us questions we didn't understand. For example, we were confused when buyers asked if we were going "DSD" (direct store delivery) or if we would offer "off-invoice, billback, or scan allowance TPRs" (temporary price reductions).

We actually lost money at times while trying to understand the different purchasing tactics some stores imposed, not knowing how each would affect us financially. We soon learned the trade of the grocery store industry. In fact, Joel became a bona fide expert in the industry as he met with buyers in huge store chains across the country. He actually became good friends with many of them.

As the product became available to more people, we received even more customer letters telling us how much they loved Kodiak Cakes. At our customers' request, we changed the packaging from a bag to a box and started selling to specialty stores, gift shops, sporting good stores, and now grocery stores across the country. After electronic communication improved via the Internet and e-mail, we started receiving customer comments almost daily from people all over the country. We loved to read each one and shared them with family members and friends.

The letters seemed to make all of the sacrifice, work, sweat, and literally tears at times worth it. Below are fifteen of the hundreds of unsolicited customer letters we have received. They tell about Kodiak Cakes in a much better way than I can:

> I am writing in regards to your Kodiak Cakes. I have two comments on this product: one good, one bad. The good news is that we love them. The bad news is that we cannot buy them in our little town of Homer, Alaska. Rita, my fiancée, was able to buy some at a store across the bay in Seldovia, but this is a one-hour boat ride away and not on our regular route, if you know what I mean. We have kept a ready store of Kodiak Cakes at my weekend place on the bay (picture of satisfied customers attached), but now, alas, we are Kodiak Cakeless .... It is a dark winter, indeed, which lies ahead holding the prospect of gnawing on the lifeless preservative -packed creations that commonly pass for pancakes these days. I'd sooner eat my own foot.
>
> *—Tom Bodett (for Motel 6), Homer Alaska*

> About two hours ago, I got off of work. My pregnant wife was upstairs and had mumbled something about being hungry. Although she mumbles A LOT about being hungry (and needing to use the restroom ... pregnancy), I thought I might surprise her with a pre-bedtime "breakfast." Especially since one of her recent cravings has been pancakes, and the last round of mix

she bought left her unsatisfied. I had purchased a box of Kodiak Cakes mix in the supermarket, just because it looked tasty. I guess it appealed to the part of me that grew up in a simpler place, the Berkshire Mountains of Massachusetts. Bottom line: bar none the best pancakes either of us has ever eaten. They tasted great, looked great, and had excellent mouthfeel. Any-who, you people got me a hug (and not much more … pregnancy). Thanks for a great product and making my wife smile.

—*Carmel, California*

Great people at Baker Mills. I found Kodiak Cakes several years ago, and for the first time in my life, I could make good pancakes and waffles. But we moved to Boston two months ago. I couldn't find them here and got some other brand. I had one bite and realized that my ability to make waffles is utterly due to your mix. So I am eating eggs until I can purchase more directly from you, or until you can let me know where they sell them here.

—*Boston, Massachusetts*

My husband had to go to Maryland to take care of my Marine stepson who was just diagnosed with lymphoma cancer (he's twenty-three). We live in Billings, Montana, and I found your Kodiak Cakes .... My husband packed a few boxes to take to Maryland for my stepson to eat while he was going through chemo (since they're so healthy). My stepson ate them for almost every meal!!! In fact, three days after chemo my stepson was up cooking them for my husband and everyone else who was there!!!!! I just wanted you to know Kodiak Cakes have helped my stepson through chemo and will continue to help him through four more treatments he has left. Thank you so much!!!! He wants ten more boxes. He's giving them out for Christmas presents.

—*Billings, Montana*

I just wanted to say your flapjacks are wonderful. As a young man I worked in logging camps on the Minnesota-Canadian border and ate flapjacks for breakfast most every morning. It was possible to buy flapjack mix in Canada. I've never seen it anywhere else. At that time you could also buy sour cream butter. It was called grade B butter. It was perfect with flapjacks and syrup. Your flapjacks bring back a flood of great memories from long ago, and I will be buying them from now on.

—*Minneapolis, Minnesota*

Dear Kodiak Pancake Mix People: If anyone asks what is the best gift we received to commemorate our sixtieth wedding anniversary, I would show the four boxes of Kodiak Pancake Mix .... The mix proved to be the best pancakes we have eaten. That is quite a compliment, since my husband as a child had pancakes almost every morning for his breakfast .... Those pancakes made with your mix are the best he has ever tasted.

—*St. George, Utah*

My son's name is Kodiak. So naturally when we stumbled across Kodiak Cakes, we had to have them. While not cheap, we find they are worth twice the price. First, the taste is fantastic! Second, the name is great! Kodiak Cakes are the only sweets we have allowed our eighteen-month-old to have. How can we refuse? He has had them for his birthday, New Year's, and now SUPER BOWL.

—*Carefree, Arizona*

My wife and I have a two-year-old who absolutely loves your Kodiak Cakes. He even got Mom and Dad hooked on the cakes. We go through about two boxes a week. We picked up the last six boxes ... about a half-hour from our house last week. It seems like they have definitely caught on in Southern California. My wife and I are rethinking conveying what a great product they are to our friends and neighbors. Now that they are all hooked the local stores are always empty. It's nice to have a healthy alternative for our son. We have a six-week-old who is a Kodiak in training. Also, your brownies are unbelievable. Thanks for putting a healthy alternative out there for breakfast; our family really enjoys the quality of your product along with the unbelievable taste.

—Dana Point, California

Several months back, my six-year-old son and I saw a box of your Kodiak Cakes on the shelf of our local supermarket. We both loved the bear and box design (old-time sourdough look) and to my surprise "just add water." And even better, no strange ingredients. We bought it and the next morning had the best pancakes ever. Every morning for six months, my son Tommy had pancakes with honey—that's all he wanted. We are really hooked on this great bear pancake.

—San Diego, California

I was never a morning person, but your Kodiak Cakes make me look forward to getting up now! I turn the griddle on … while it's warming up, I measure out one cup of water, one cup mix, and in a few minutes, my family is sitting down to a healthy, delicious breakfast. Your pancake mix is simply the best there is. The ingredients are so nutritious you have enough energy to sail well into the afternoon before feeling hungry. With any other breakfast, I was always hungry an hour later. My son, Skyler, gave me the "best mom in the world" comment. (Shhhhh, they still think I get up early and cook from scratch ... ha ha!) A great big thank you from me!

—Corte Madera, California

I just wanted to tell you that your pancakes are wonderful! But more important than that, I ate them on my low glycemic diet every morning with a no-sugar maple syrup and was able to lose fifty pounds.

—Torrance, California

We cannot tell you how much we love the Kodiak Cakes. My cousin, who lives in McHenry, IL, served them for breakfast …. One bite, we were hooked. My husband and I recently lost over twenty pounds and have been particularly concerned about the "white" carbs. I think eliminating them from our diet was the biggest cause of the weight loss. Kodiak Cakes prove that you don't sacrifice taste with the absence of white flour. We have them twice a week for breakfast without having gained an ounce back. And when we discovered the Kodiak Brownies, I thought I'd died and gone to heaven! Without a doubt, the BEST brownies I've ever had. Thanks so much for a terrific product.

—Madison, Iowa

First, I would like to thank your company for making a wonderful product! I live in the marshes of south Louisiana in a small town named Houma .... I turned diabetic at the turn of the century and have found that most of the products made for diabetics are either overpriced, overpromoted, or just plain overrated! I came across your Kodiak Cakes mix at Rouse's Foods in Houma. They were so good, along with having a high amount of fiber, that I went back and bought all of the boxes that they had. Since then I had my wife get online and order a case from y'all because the store had not restocked your mix. Not only do I make my waffles plain, I also make chocolate, chocolate with peanut butter, peanut butter, blueberry flavored, and raspberry flavored. It has added a great amount of flavor and diversity to an otherwise restricted diet, and I don't fill like I am cheating .... Many thanks!!

—Houma, Louisiana

Dear Kodiak Cakes, I have used your pancake mix for the last several years and found it to be even better than my own wonderful homemade recipe. Then when I saw that you had a brownie mix, I knew that it would be the right blend: not too sweet, great texture, incredible taste, and nutritionally sound. And of course, it was. Now I am in love with your brownies and consider them better than my homemade. Having had a wholesomely homemade restaurant for a few years, I think that is a tremendous compliment. Keep up the perfect work! And my hat is off to you. Thanks for making baking/cooking ever so much easier for me. Please broaden your product line. I beg you! Because you get it all right.

—Mill Valley, California

I am sixty-five years old and have tried many "natural" pancake and waffle mixes over the years and have never tasted a lighter, more delicious pancake than yours. I have a very rich and good brownie recipe, from the "Elegant But Easy" cookbook, but since your pancakes were so good, I thought I would try the brownie mix.

> Well, no pun intended, yours takes the cake. The brownies are dense, moist, and absolutely homemade tasting .... I will recommend your products to everyone I know!
>
> —*Philadelphia, Pennsylvania*

As we continued to expand our sales, we decided to begin using some of our revenue to advertise on the radio. As with every other decision, we spent a lot of time researching which radio station would be best, what times of day to air the marketing spots, and what kind of spots we should use. Since we couldn't afford to produce an expensive commercial, Joel wrote some text that the radio hosts would read and talk about live on the air. We finally decided on one radio station and were able to negotiate outstanding rates with their sales representative. A couple of times Joel cooked up some pancakes at the radio station and took them to the show hosts so they could eat and talk about them while on the air.

As with other vendors, my negotiating skills pretty much consisted of this plea: "We are a small start-up company and have no money, so can you please give us your best price? As we grow we would like to purchase more of your products and services." It was the truth and it worked. As anticipated, the radio spots helped us create a strong local customer base, so we used the radio as much as we could afford.

However, when we were out of marketing dollars, we still

needed to do more promotion, but we didn't have the money. Joel decided to contact newspapers, magazines, radio stations, and news channels to see if he could get stories about Baker Mills and Kodiak Cakes out for free. That worked too. Soon newspapers and magazines published stories about Kodiak Cakes. Joel was also cooking up pancakes on local television morning shows. I did two television spots with Joel, but Joel was a natural in front of the camera. In fact, over the next decade, Joel would be on all the local television channels at least thirty times, cooking pancakes and other recipes made out of our Kodiak Cakes mix, such as cookies and cakes. I remember during our second show the cameraman was eating Kodiak Cakes while holding a plate of them in one hand and maneuvering the camera with the other. Joel also looked for free radio marketing opportunities on sporting and outdoor radio shows—and got them. Getting into the media this way saved us thousands of dollars and helped ignite sales and build the brand.

Joel and I also promoted Kodiak Cakes in other ways. We demonstrated Kodiak Cakes in grocery stores, cooked them at special events and functions, and gave away hundreds of boxes for people to try. Joel even gave away two cases of Kodiak Cakes during a half-time football game at our former high school to the person who kicked the longest field goal. I still remember thinking, *What if none of the contestants pulled from the stadium make a field goal—then what will Joel do?* But as luck had it, one kid kicked a darn long field goal, and we all breathed more easily as the announcer told the crowd he had just won two cases of Kodiak Cakes.

Once I was asked to cook Kodiak Cakes for the Utah State Senate and House of Representatives during their January legislative meetings. I remember hearing a couple of hungry politicians coming into the break room and asking others, "Where do we get some of those 'Klondike Cakes' to eat?" I thought it was funny watching many of the politicians leave the assembly rooms right in the middle of speeches and discussions to eat pancakes. I also headed up a Boy Scout fundraiser in which the Scouts sold a bunch of Kodiak Cakes door to door in Park City, Utah.

Although seeing Kodiak Cakes succeed was fabulous, it was nevertheless hard work, and we still weren't making the amount of money we hoped for. All the money we received had to go right back into the company. Because of this, I had to keep working full time for another organization. Soon, however, the stress and finances were too much for me to keep Kodiak Cakes going. I was working full time, getting my master's degree, serving as a Boy Scout leader, and heading up Baker Mills. I was also a father with a family that meant very much to me. Finally I just couldn't keep up anymore.

So at the end of 1997, I offloaded the company to Joel, who was eager to take it on. It was a great decision. Joel is a natural salesman, marketer, and entrepreneur. People love Joel because he is smart and honest and has fabulous personal relations skills. As the new president of Baker Mills and half owner, Joel incorporated the business. Up until then it was a sole proprietorship in my name. Joel sacrificed a great deal for the company and invested much of his own money as he continued to increase sales.

As sales increased we outgrew our original manufacturing company, which could no longer keep up with the volume. Our second manufacturing company couldn't sustain the quality we desired. The third went out of business. The fourth was remarkable but eventually charged us too much to produce Kodiak Cakes. We finally changed to a fifth manufacturer—Lehi Roller Mills, where, coincidentally, Grandpa had worked nearly a hundred years earlier as a young teenager.

As we sold to grocery stores, we were surprised to find that most grocery store chains wanted to carry our product. We were so excited. However, since getting into grocery stores required a lot of money up front, we couldn't grow as fast as we hoped. When selling to grocery stores, we were commonly charged a "slotting" fee—which took some getting used to! A slotting fee is the amount a store chain charges per product per store to carry a new item. We tried everything we could to negotiate a way out of paying slotting fees. We offered not to pay the fee, to pay less than the amount requested, to put the money into marketing instead, or just give the chain free product instead of cash. Often we were successful.

In addition to slotting fees, we found that once we were in a store chain, we had to sell a lot of product or we would be discontinued. Grocery stores need to move the product they have on their shelves to bring in revenue. In order to move product, we had to market and promote Kodiak Cakes. This meant that we had to sink money into grocery store ads, end-aisle displays, and food demos. It cost a fortune. Slotting fees, marketing costs, and the expense of producing Kodiak Cakes for a new chain were so costly that we had to delay getting into some chains—often for several years until we could get the money.

One day we couldn't wait any longer with a particular local store chain that we had put off for three years. Since we didn't have any money, we decided to approach a neighbor who had offered to invest in our company. Luck was on our side again as Joel and I met with him. He invested $13,000 in the company for 6.5 percent ownership. Though it was hard to give up a slice of the company, we had to do it. It proved to be a good decision, as the store chain sold a lot of the product, and we were able to eventually earn enough money to buy our shares back from him a few years later.

When we approached him several years later to see if we could buy our shares back, we were astounded when he only wanted his original $13,000 back and refused to take any interest. He told us he just wanted to help us succeed. We were in shock. He was a very successful entrepreneur himself and said he just wanted our company to succeed. We were and will always be so grateful and humbled by his generosity. In fact, the only thing he asked for during the several years he owned the 6.5 percent was a case or two of Kodiak Cakes each Christmas to give to friends. I still can't believe his kindness.

In 2001 Joel left for Oxford University in England to pursue a master's degree in business administration. This is actually a great story, because when Joel was in high school there was some anxiety over his grades. As a junior, Joel was dismissed from the football team because of bad grades. To get him back on the team, our dad convinced a teacher to let Joel make up one of his grades. When Joel went to college, he made a 180-degree turn. He graduated magna cum laude in economics from the University of Utah and was later accepted to Oxford University. He followed our older brother Tim's example—Tim was an academic all-American football player at Brigham Young University and an Oxford PhD. Tim showed us that it was important to do well in school while having fun on the gridiron. But I have to say that our mom and dad gave us the vision for doing well in college so doors would be open to us later in life. Dad had obtained a PhD from the University of Southern California in preparation for his career in teaching.

When Joel left for Oxford he gave the oversight of the company back to me for a year. However, since I was now working for a consulting firm and was frequently out of town, Joel hired a student from the University of Utah to operate the company while Joel was away. Our employee did a fabulous job managing Baker Mills until Joel returned home after completing his degree to once again take it over.

After Joel came home, he had to find additional employment

to make enough money to support his family while running Baker Mills. Unfortunately the company still wasn't providing enough income to meet his needs. But Joel worked at it and kept growing the business. It wasn't easy, though, as he worked multiple jobs. In fact, many times he grew so tired that he wondered if we should sell the company or just close it. On several occasions he said he would give the company six more months and then see. At the end of each six-month period he just kept going.

A couple of years later, in 2003, Dad had retired as a professor and decided to help Joel. Dad became Joel's vice president and was a terrific burst of energy and insight, precisely what Joel needed. Dad is a mover and shaker and a fun person to work with. When we were young we painted houses in the summers with him for a couple years. He was our best friend, and we learned to work hard from his example.

Together Joel and Dad moved the "international headquarters" of Baker Mills, as Dad liked to call it, to my parents' basement. It was great to see them at work during the day in my parents' home with computers, papers, and files all over the place. Upstairs, their kitchen soon became a food lab, where they and Mom worked on developing new products.

During this time Joel created a fabulous company Internet site, which allowed customers to start buying Kodiak Cakes and other Baker Mills products online. Joel and Dad also increased Kodiak Cakes distribution to many more grocery store chains, specialty stores, and sporting good stores all over the country. They attended large national food shows to promote Baker Mills products and flew to different states to meet with grocery store chain buyers. The buyers enjoyed meeting with Dad and talking to him on the phone because he is so friendly and personable. He would also speak with customers on the phone for several minutes, just talking to them as though they were longtime friends. Dad's ability to relate with others is amazing, which was in part why he decided to be a professor.

Joel and Dad next paid a company to develop the ingredients for three delicious Kodiak Cakes syrups: raspberry, apple cider, and marionberry. Joel and Dad even bought a huge kettle to make the syrups themselves in a kitchen they leased. However, it became too much work, so they decided to outsource the production of their syrups. Over the next year they exchanged the apple cider syrup for strawberry and then again to mountain berry, which became a big hit.

In 2006, after a full year of development, Joel and Dad introduced Big Bear Brownies—a delicious brownie mix made with 100 percent whole wheat flour. I remember going to my parents' home and sampling batch after batch of freshly made brownies. As with Kodiak Cakes, their hard work paid off, and Big Bear Brownies became another successful Baker Mills product. Soon after the brownies went to market, we began to again experience the delight of receiving many customer letters telling us how much they loved the product. One customer from Madison, Iowa, for example, wrote, "When we discovered the Kodiak Brownies, I thought I'd died and gone to heaven!

Without a doubt, the best brownies I've ever had." Another customer from Westminster, Maryland wrote, "We just tried your Big Bear Brownies and they are the richest, moistest, most decadent brownies we have ever tasted from a mix. It won't be worth making them from scratch anymore! Thanks for making a delicious, good-for-you, treat!"

In February 2007, an ultimate event for a food manufacturer took place. Kodiak Cakes was featured on the front cover of *Bon Appétit* magazine, one of the biggest food magazines in the country. This thrilling event brought nationwide publicity that helped increase sales. In 2009 Joel launched Bear Country Cookies, an incredibly delicious oatmeal dark chocolate cookie, made with 100 percent whole wheat flour. Also in 2009, Joel made plans to open a Kodiak Cakes Bear Country Cookies store at a popular Salt Lake City mall, our company's first outlet store.

Over the years Baker Mills has continued to grow as a family business, with all of our products remaining true to Mom's original strategy of using only the finest and most wholesome ingredients available. Whole grains are especially important to us, since Grandpa and Mom believed that nutrition was as important as taste. The experience has been fun though rigorous and challenging. Through the difficult years, we sometimes wondered if it was all worth it. I think we can finally say that indeed it was. What did we learn through the years of creating and marketing the Kodiak Cakes brand? Specifically, there are ten lessons I think every entrepreneur must learn and apply to help ensure his or her success.

LESSON ONE: ARE YOU PREPARED?

As you most likely anticipate, starting a company is an exciting and exhilarating career opportunity. Unique and distinctive from other vocations, such as the corporate employee whose work is often tied to a specific function within a large enterprise, the entrepreneur enjoys a diverse and holistic approach to business. In this setting the entrepreneur directly addresses all business areas, such as strategy, management, operations, finance, accounting, marketing, and sales.

In addition, while most careers impose limits on income levels, the entrepreneur is generally free from monetary caps. Not only does this advantage result in potentially high income levels, but it also creates an inherent performance incentive, propelling the entrepreneur into satisfying heights of achievement and accomplishment. The entrepreneur also enjoys the flexibility of being independent from a "boss," an arrangement seldom experienced in other careers.

Despite these and other advantages to starting your own company, being an entrepreneur is nevertheless a career. As such, it should be treated like any other career that requires essential preparation for success. Some individuals, however, erroneously perceive entrepreneurship and the American dream as a means of getting rich quickly or getting something for nothing. Nothing could be farther from truth.

As with all professions, whether nursing, law, architecture, or education, starting your own company requires proper and essential preparation. While it is true that some successful entrepreneurs did not carefully prepare or formally train for their career, they are exceptions to the rule. Even then, many of these unique entrepreneurs may not have fully optimized the success they could have achieved if they had prepared better. And since 90 percent of business startups fail, obtaining the proper preparation is most crucial.

So how does an aspiring entrepreneur who is naturally suited and passionate about this career choice prepare? There are four primary ways:

- Learn core business fundamentals, particularly accounting
- Interview other entrepreneurs
- Study other organizations
- Gain experience with other organizations

When I was young I asked many successful entrepreneurs

what they thought I should study in college to help prepare me to start my own company. Unequivocally, I was told by each to study accounting. They said I needed to know how to "read the books" or the financial statements of the company, i.e., the income statement, balance sheet, and cash flow statement.

Accordingly, I took their advice to heart and obtained a bachelor of science degree in accounting from the University of Utah. This discipline was definitely not my passion, nor did it come as easily to me as it did to many of my classmates. In fact, during the accounting courses I took, I often wondered if I should change my major to marketing, which more closely resembled my personality. Fortunately I stayed with accounting so I could be better equipped to start my own company.

After my bachelor's degree I gained four additional years of work experience while employed with a large manufacturing company. The founder and owner of the company was a notable philanthropist, Obert Clark Tanner. While he was young he went to school and obtained his PhD. Education was very important to him. It was a coincidence that he was a relative of mine, yet I learned greater insight into why he was such a successful and well-respected man. While employed by his company, I worked in marketing research, auditing, and operations improvement and learned all I could. In 1994, at the latter end of my employment there, I started Baker Mills as a side business.

With the goal of obtaining more education, I went back to the University of Utah in 1996 to obtain my master of business administration with an emphasis in entrepreneurship. This additional education put the finishing touches on the academic preparation I needed. I took more specialized businesses classes, such as new product development, strategy, problem solving, organizational behavior, and consulting, which prepared me to start my own company.

After completing all the entrepreneurship courses the business school offered, I asked the dean of the business school if I could design two additional, entrepreneurship-related classes to fill two electives. He consented with the caveat that I obtained sponsoring professors and approval from the department faculty director.

As part of one of these courses, I interviewed a handful of extremely successful multimillionaire entrepreneurs, including one self-made billionaire in the petrochemical industry, Jon M. Huntsman. From these entrepreneurs I wanted to learn what they attributed their success to, how they acquired capital to start their businesses, what pitfalls to avoid, the preparation required, and other general advice for starting a company.

Regarding preparation, Mr. Huntsman told me, "A successful entrepreneur must be well disciplined in all key business areas, such as marketing, finance, and accounting." In addition to formal academic training, Mr. Huntsman said, "Learning to be a great entrepreneur requires being taught by those who wear the moccasins." He is also known for saying, "Go learn for ten years on someone else's dime." I learned that Mr. Huntsman had obtained his bachelor's degree in economics, from

The Wharton School of Business at the University of Pennsylvania, and he later earned his MBA from the University of Southern California.

Other entrepreneurs made similar comments. For instance, one said, "You must have a good basis in business fundamentals."

Another advised, "I recommend getting a good degree like an accounting degree and an MBA or a finance degree and an MBA or an engineering degree and MBA."

A third said, "I think you need to know the basics in accounting and have a good math background."

While I believe all the education you can get is best, which would include obtaining a strong bachelor's degree and an MBA, at a minimum an entrepreneur should at least learn the core business fundamentals, even if through personal study. Core business disciplines typically include accounting, finance, marketing, management, strategy, operations, business law, operations, and economics. Other courses are also basic to a good business education as well, such as information systems, human resources, organizational behavior, and leadership. The more education you can acquire the better. In fact, advanced math, writing, and communications courses will also help you prepare for your career as an entrepreneur.

Beyond obtaining a formal education and conducting personal interviews, I read books on business startups and how different organizations became successful. I also toured other companies to get a feel for their operations and culture and talked to a number of business administrators. In addition, I found that working for other organizations provided a great foundation for becoming an entrepreneur. While working for other organizations, I had the opportunity to use what I learned and to observe firsthand how companies operated and how leaders led. Quality work experience for a company in the industry in which you want to start a business provides especially good training. For example, before starting Baker Mills I worked for a high-end specialty food distributor, which gave me valuable industry-specific experience.

Concerning work experience, one of the entrepreneurs I interviewed told me, "Get experience in an operating environment in a big company. I think it is better to start out in a big company and then move to a small company, where you can get lots of experience. If you do the reverse and start out in a small company, you may not get good experience at first. But big, successful companies teach you right. Then go to a small company for broader experience."

LESSON TWO: THE FOUR "Ps" OF ENTREPRENEURSHIP

After you have sufficiently prepared, you must then take on the next four "Ps" of entrepreneurship: perseverance, product, passion, and profitability. You must understand and apply each one to become successful.

PERSEVERANCE

Do you have what it takes to start a company? The first lesson I learned from my experience with Kodiak Cakes was that entrepreneurship is not for the fainthearted. Mr. Huntsman told me clearly that being an entrepreneur "is the toughest and most difficult occupation."

Another highly successful entrepreneur told me that some are unsuccessful in starting their companies because "Number one, they are unwilling to pay the price." A successful entrepreneur from a high-tech industry said to me, "You must have a not-giving-up attitude. It takes diligent persistence, work, and hard struggles."

For most entrepreneurs, starting a company is a painfully difficult process at best. The required sacrifice, commitment, investment, and opportunity costs can be overwhelming. I recall one entrepreneur saying he literally worked eighty hours a week and only took home $6,000 a year in salary during his first years.

One day, after starting Baker Mills, I walked downstairs into my unfinished basement, into the space where my raw ingredients and finished inventory were stored. I was emotionally, financially, and physically spent. As I walked into the room, I looked at the neatly stacked cases of Kodiak Cakes inventory. I thought of the countless hours and money I had put into launching the business. I thought of how tight we were financially and wondered why the journey had been so hard and why we weren't making more money. We were poor.

In stress and exhaustion I broke down. I tearfully picked up a thirty-pound case of Kodiak Cakes and threw it into the corner of the room against the cement basement wall as hard as I could. The box broke open, spilling out the two-and-a-half-pound packages inside. I picked up another case and threw it against the wall as well. I threw about eight more and then sat down on the fifty-pound bags of dry milk and sobbed. I had given everything I could to this company. But it wasn't making money as quickly as I needed it to. I couldn't do anymore. I was drained from the late nights and overwork. As I sat there on the bags with my head down, I thought I could see in my mind's eye my Grandpa and Grandma, who had passed away many years before, looking at me in their calm, reassuring manner. After some time I got up, left the room, and went back to work.

After another year, however, the stress of so many demands became unbearable, and out of sheer exhaustion I decided I needed to shut down the company. I couldn't keep up with everything. I couldn't afford to pay anyone to help me, either. I once tried to sell the company to a massive multibillion-dollar company. However, they decided we were too small to purchase. It was at this time that my brother Joel expressed some interest in running Baker Mills and taking it off my hands. It was the perfect hand off. So, as I previously mentioned, at the end of 1997 I turned my company over to Joel. It was like passing the baton to a fellow teammate after running a very long race.

After Joel took over the company, he began to feel similar struggles—barely having enough money to support his family, working alone day after day and year after year, wondering when real success would come. Some friends of ours started companies and found success long before we did. After a couple of years Joel also wondered if he should keep the company going or sell it. It would actually be more than a decade before he would really see significant success.

PRODUCT

If you have what it takes to be an entrepreneur, then it is time to determine what industry you want to work in and what product you will sell. Product simply represents your business idea. While technically a product is something tangible, in practice many people refer to both products and services as simply products. For instance, a consulting company may have three services they sell: strategic planning, operations improvement, and change management. However, while these are each technically consulting services, many term them products or product lines. In the health care industry, hospitals refer to their patient services or service lines—such as cardiology, neurology, orthopedics, radiology, and pediatrics—as products and product lines.

Once you have the idea of what kind of product you want to sell, you should ask yourself some important initial questions: Is this a reasonable product to sell? Will people buy this product? Or simply, is this a good idea? The best way to answer these questions is to ask potential customers for their opinions and feedback.

This approach is referred to as being "market-driven" as opposed to being "sales-driven." A market-driven approach discovers what the market wants and builds a product around that need. It gives potential customers the opportunity to express their opinions and provide you with valuable feedback that can help shape your product. On the other hand, a sales-driven approach tells the market what you have to offer and communicates to the customers that they need to buy your product. A sales-driven company is less flexible because it does not consider the opinions of the market. While in some cases a sales-driven model can work, a market-driven model is far more likely to succeed.

With Baker Mills and our first product, Kodiak Cakes, I procured feedback from various people. I asked if they liked the taste of the product, the name, the pricing, weight, package dimensions, and the packaging design. As we received feedback we made modifications. As Baker Mills grew and expanded over the years, we continued to ask consumers what they wanted and how we should shape our products. We listened. In fact, based on a consumer survey we conducted, we developed a brownie mix as our second product.

While the concept of being market-driven and delivering great products into the hands of consumers seems intuitive, it is nevertheless surprising that so many products appear to be in "draft" form or still in beta testing. Have you ever purchased a food product that tasted awful and wondered how it ever made it to market? It's kind of like seeing a TV commercial and wondering who in their right mind produced it—and worse, who approved it to air on TV. Or perhaps you have passed by a billboard on the highway that contained so much text that you couldn't read it all, or the font was way too small to read.

Some companies seem to totally disregard their customers

when developing products. Once, after purchasing a high-end mountain bike from a popular bike manufacturer, I found several performance flaws. I was amazed the bike got to market—I surely didn't enjoy riding it. Way too many products on the market, from cars to refrigerators, seem defective in design or quality. I wonder how these products got to market and if the companies that produced them asked enough consumers for their opinions during the product development stage.

The reason a market-driven approach is so important is that as bright and brilliant as you might be, chances are you are not objective enough to determine what the market really wants. Too many entrepreneurs are so excited about their ideas that they don't enlist the opinions and feedback of others. Nor do they take the time to refine their products before they begin selling them.

Now a word of caution: some ideas are so clever and innovative that they should be kept confidential until they reach the market. You must avoid the risk of someone stealing your idea. This presents a delicate dilemma in terms of being market-driven. If you can't talk openly about your product you will have to covertly investigate and research the market without disclosing the specifics of your product.

PASSION

Make sure you are passionate about both the industry in which you want to start your business and the product you wish to sell. A multimillionaire entrepreneur told me, "Look for the right industry and company.... It's got to be right for you. You have got to like the industry." Passion is the fuel that generates strong motivation behind your venture. In addition, you must have a passion for the reason you are starting the business. The cause is what keeps the entrepreneur going. It represents the mission and driving force behind hard work, perseverance, and ultimate success.

One millionaire entrepreneur told me, "We stay focused on our mission and not on the money. The money must never be the focal point. If it becomes that, you are two to three years away from extinction. I'm not in this for the money."

Making money just for the sake of making money may not provide enough fulfillment and passion to start, grow, and maintain a successful company. However, making money can definitely be inspiring if the motive behind it is to make a better life for yourself and others—encapsulated in the American dream. Starting a company is too hard if the purpose is just to make money. It would be easier to work for someone else for a paycheck.

Great entrepreneurs are driven by something they are passionate about and the underlying causes behind those passions. Mr. Huntsman, a billionaire, as I mentioned, told me, "I am motivated by charitable causes. I make money to give it away." He has given $100 million to cancer research and millions of dollars to other charitable, community, and education causes.

I was passionate about the food industry and the whole-grain products we wanted to sell. I love food, grocery stores, and baked goods. I love the feel of fifty-pound flour sacks. I like to look at them, sit on them, and carry them. So when Mom gave me the idea to start Baker Mills, I was delighted. Trying to develop the best and highest quality pancake and waffle mix was problem solving that inherently gave me an exciting and motivating quest.

In addition, I had to be an entrepreneur. I needed the freedom of working for myself, to be creative and have the opportunity to perform at my highest level. Another underlying cause for me to start the company was to make a better life for others. This provided an important purpose that helped me persevere.

PROFITABILITY

The fourth "P" is profitability. You have to make money. When our Kodiak Cakes mix was ready for market, I didn't want to overcharge customers. I was concerned that my prices could be too high because the ingredients we used were so expensive. However, when I talked to a self-made millionaire entrepreneur friend of mine from the food industry, he said, "Do not be afraid to make money." My margins were so thin that I wasn't sure I would be able to stay in business long.

Another entrepreneur explained to me that many people

are unsuccessful when starting their own businesses because "They fail at getting margins and knowing how important that is. So we sold [our product] at a hundred percent markup." We could never come close to that high of a markup in the food industry, where money is made on volume. However, the point is that you must make money not only to survive, but also to flourish, expand, become competitive, and stay viable.

Your margins and profitability must be considered long before you actually start your company and lay out any cash. This means you must make financial projections to see if your business can make money or not. If you can't make money, you simply must abandon your business idea and conceive a new one.

Financial projections, including a break-even analysis, are essential; they are also quite simple and straightforward to conduct. Unfortunately, however, I doubt whether many start-ups go through this exercise, since so many don't make money and subsequently close their doors. Therefore, let me quickly take you through these basic financial calculations. This is a somewhat technical section, and not as fun to read, though absolutely imperative for success. So hold on and push through the next few pages!

First, in building financial projections for your company, all you are doing is projecting your monthly revenue and costs over a three-to-five-year timeline (preferably five). Each year you will update these three-to-five-year projections with new information to keep them accurate. Financial projections are developed by *conservatively* estimating the volumes of your product you think you will sell on a monthly basis. If you have a host of products, then you can either forecast the sales of each one, or you can estimate an overall total volume for all products pooled together.

Suppose you plan to open a bookstore. Rather than individually projecting sales for each book, you could just estimate a total monthly volume of books sold, such as thirty books a day initially, or approximately 900 books a month (assuming an average of thirty days of business per month for easier calculations). Next, carry this estimate out over three to five years, adjusting for month-to-month growth potential. You might believe your book volumes will increase 1 percent a month for the first year. Years two and three may grow at an annual rate of 4 percent and 5 percent, respectively, divided evenly over each twelve-month period.

After you project your volumes over three to five years, then estimate your revenue. Begin by estimating the price you think you can get for each unit sold. Again, if you have multiple products to sell, you can estimate an average price per unit sold. Suppose you think your average book price would be twenty dollars. Then multiply your volumes by the price to generate your monthly revenue projections. Carry this out over three to five years, accounting for inflation (perhaps 3 percent per year) or other factors that may increase your price from year to year.

Next determine your costs. Costs are determined in two

parts. The first part is known as direct or variable costs. These costs are associated with the cost of each product. Such costs increase as volumes increase. Said another way, direct costs consist of the direct materials and direct labor required to produce a single unit. These costs change based on the volume produced or sold.

It is often easier to include only the cost of materials, since labor costs often remain unchanged, regardless of how many products or units you sell. Next, multiply your direct cost by your projected monthly sales volumes to get your total monthly direct costs. Estimate any cost increases from year to year as well (such as 3 % annually for inflation).

In the bookstore example, your average direct cost may include only the cost of the books (or cost of goods sold). In this case, the average cost may be ten dollars (50 percent of the sales price). Labor costs would most likely be excluded, since the bookstore may employ staff who are paid a set salary regardless of how many books are sold.

The second part of calculating costs is to estimate all other costs required to operate your company. These are known as indirect or fixed costs, because they don't change in relation to volumes—or the number of units sold. Fixed costs may include labor as well as overhead (i.e., rent, lights, heat, and water), insurance, property taxes, salaries, marketing expenses, licensing fees, and interest payments. Estimate these costs from month to month and year to year, adjusting for any projected cost increases (such as an annual 3 percent inflation increase). After your indirect or fixed costs have been estimated, add them to your direct or variable costs to get a total cost for each month. Project this total out over your three-to-five-year timeline.

Next, subtract your estimated total costs from your estimated total revenue for each month. What you have left is either a positive or negative number, indicating a gain or loss. The gain is known as gross income. If you have gross income left over, estimate your taxes and deduct that amount. The difference represents your net income.

Some people talk about EBITDA (pronounced ē-bit-dă). Don't let this term confuse you. It just means earnings before interest, taxes, depreciation, and amortization. To get to this number, all you do is add your interest payments, taxes, depreciation, and amortization back to your net income. EBITDA is a metric often used to determine profitability from operations, particularly for companies with large capital costs. Though many people refer to this important number, don't worry about it initially. It's not a "generally accepted accounting principle" metric.

Regarding your financial projections, I am an advocate of conducting three different projection scenarios: one representing worst case, one representing best case, and one for expected case. In each of these models you need to adjust your volume projections as well as your pricing and costs to reflect different cases. If your worst case scenario is still earning you enough income, you may have an excellent venture to pursue. If not you may need to rethink pursuing it.

Now calculate your break-even point. This just means how

many units of your product you must sell to cover your costs so that you have no loss or gain. I cannot emphasize how critical it is to calculate your break-even point before you start your company. Think of all the companies that go under because they didn't know in advance how many pizzas or cars they needed to sell each day or month to cover their costs. Far too many companies can't sell enough of their product to cover their costs after they open their doors.

To calculate the break-even point, simply estimate your monthly indirect or fixed costs and divide that number by the gross margin you will receive on your product. For example, for the bookstore, the average cost per book is ten dollars and the average price you think you will get is twenty dollars. Taking the difference between these two numbers gives you ten dollars, which is the gross margin you will receive on your product. If your indirect, or fixed, costs are estimated at $10,000 per month, then how many books do you need to sell each month to break even? The answer is about 1,000 a month ($10,000 fixed costs / $10 margin per unit)—or roughly thirty-three books per day (1,000 books a month / thirty days). Can you sell that many books in a month? In this example, we initially estimated sales of thirty books a day or 900 books a month. So this company will start off losing money because it projected it can only sell thirty rather than thirty-three books a day.

However, since most businesses lose money up front due to start-up costs and the time required to generate a customer base, you also need to know in advance when you can cover your costs. This is easily done by looking at the bottom line on your monthly financial projections until you find the month in which your losses turn into net income, or when your revenues equal your costs. In the bookstore example, it will break even in month twelve. This is based on the projection that it will sell 900 books in month one, 909 books in month two, 919 books in month three, until it sells 1,004 books in month twelve (based on the 1 percent monthly sales increase projected during the first year of business).

LESSON THREE: DO YOUR HOMEWORK?

Many people associate entrepreneurship with high risk taking. However, entrepreneurship depends not so much on ordinary risk taking as on calculated risk taking—a much different term. Calculated risk taking means you have as much information as you can reasonably acquire to help you make prudent decisions, particularly investment decisions.

When a person is confused about which of two directions to take, he usually just needs more information to make the right decision. Information is what reduces risk and transforms an ordinary risk into a calculated one. Mr. Huntsman told me, "People must take risks—well-thought-out and well-defined calculated risks. Risk involves homework and understanding the marketplace. Risk taking is really not risk taking to me at all. Risk taking is a matter of wise investment."

From my observation, unsuccessful entrepreneurs usually do not have enough information to make informed decisions because they have not done enough homework. Emotions often get in the way, as startups are hastily undertaken without having studied all available information. Customers are not interviewed, consumer purchasing trends are not studied, financial projections are not performed, too much money is impulsively borrowed, capital equipment is purchased too quickly, and so on. Every decision, particularly in the beginning stages of a company, must be right.

New companies are in a delicate state with limited financing. Because of this there is little margin for error. In fact you simply cannot afford to make big mistakes. To minimize the risk of making such mistakes, you must do your research. I conduct research to the point of diminishing returns—when performing additional research no longer provides value.

When I started Baker Mills I had very little money. In fact, as I mentioned earlier, my only seed money was the $1,400 I earned from buying and selling a used pickup truck. Because of my limited capital I could not afford to make poor purchasing decisions. Spending mistakes could have stopped my company dead in its tracks. So I was forced to research everything I purchased to start the company. I looked at every possible avenue before spending a single dollar. When I made up my mind to spend money on a particular purchase, I negotiated the pricing as low as possible.

Not long after I started Baker Mills, Joel and I handed out surveys to consumers in grocery store parking lots. I studied at length the food industry and consumer food trends. I identified which states in the United States to penetrate first. I studied options to produce Kodiak Cakes in the most cost-effective manner. I researched every competitor I could identify and learned about their financial statements, how long they had been in business, and what products they offered. Every decision I made was based on extensive information gathering.

Even when all the homework is done, however, you are still walking out into the dark. However, you should have a pretty good idea that you will be safe and find your footing. You should feel assured that you will have a market that will buy your product. After all the homework I had done with Baker Mills, I felt the calculated risks were worth taking and came to the conclusion that I'd rather start the company and step into the dark, knowing that I could fail, than not try at all. My homework deeply diminished my risk. It didn't altogether eliminate it.

One entrepreneur told me, "Maintain the realization that things might not work out, and don't be overly disappointed if they don't. Some people don't accept that. You need a high dose of reality. Some starts just don't work. You need to have a good idea and feel good about it. Then you can continue to be persistent about it." The key is to do your homework before you start your business so you can reasonably project whether it will succeed. But even after you open your doors, wise entrepreneurs frequently incorporate "reality checks" into their business startups to determine if their business is a swan or a duck. If a swan, they continue to aggressively move forward; if a duck, they pull out and look for other possibilities.

When you have done your homework, don't let fear get in the way and restrain your desire and ability to move forward. For those emerging entrepreneurial spirits who desire to consummate the American dream, perhaps the stirring words of President Theodore Roosevelt will provide the catalyst to begin the venture of what Jon M. Huntsman christened "the most noble occupation," the entrepreneur. "Far better it is to dare mighty things, to win glorious triumphs, even though checkered by failure, than to take rank with those poor spirits who neither enjoy nor suffer much, because they live in that twilight that knows not victory nor defeat."

LESSON FOUR: DEVELOP AND STICK TO YOUR STRATEGY

You should never officially start your company and step out into the dark until you have devised a sound business strategy. Developing your strategy involves sifting through all the information you have acquired as you have learned about your product, your industry, market, competitors, suppliers, manufacturing options, regulations, and so forth, to determine how you can optimize short- and long-term sales and profits. Your strategy is your game plan—how you will compete to win.

Strategy is based upon being either a low-cost provider or differentiating your product from competitive products in some way. A low-cost provider strategy means you will provide a product similar to what the market already has, but you will do so for a better price. A product differentiation strategy means you have a new or different product to offer the market. Some businesses differentiate themselves by offering superior customer service, being in closer proximity to customers, or by offering a product that is higher in quality, easier to purchase, or easier to use.

Whichever strategy you decide to pursue—whether low cost or product differentiation—the objective is to give customers an effective reason to buy your product instead of competitive products. A highly successful entrepreneur told me. "If you are going to make cornflakes, you better have more than just plain cornflakes to offer. Otherwise, how will you draw consumers to your brand?"

At Baker Mills, our strategy was to provide the most delicious, healthy, and convenient whole grain food mix products. That strategy worked, and we stuck to it. We would not cheapen our ingredients for increased profit and thus compromise on taste, nutrition, and convenience. Furthermore, we would not be allured into other business opportunities that would dilute our effort. We would focus on our core strategy.

Too many entrepreneurs become initially successful within the confines of their business strategy, only to later stray away from it to pursue seemingly small tangents if not altogether new ideas. Unfortunately, they often lose traction in their core business as sales flatten or decline, while simultaneously being unsuccessful on their add-on ventures. Many entrepreneurs live a roller coaster lifestyle and begin venture after venture—some that win and others that lose.

To me this roller-coaster pattern isn't entrepreneurship as much as it is deal making. I'm not a deal maker. That is too risky for me, because it is like gambling. It seems counterintuitive to invest the required time and effort into so many different ventures when just one venture can consume so many resources. Some individuals are good at it, though it's just not my core competency.

Another renowned entrepreneur told me, "People who think they got the Midas touch go off into other ventures and lose everything. I can name many people whom that has happened to. The key is to focus on what you are good at. Just because you are successful in cars does not mean you will be successful in computers. Stick to the knitting."

Along with formulating your strategy is formulating the mission and vision of your business, which gets back to the passion of your business. Even though much has been written on the value of establishing a company's mission and vision, they are often overlooked. Basically, the mission states the purpose of the company, and the vision states the overall long-term objective of the business. These concepts place the company on a path that gives it a reason to exist. The strategy, on the other hand, describes in detail how the business will achieve its mission and long-term vision.

My brother Joel stated, "Once you have formulated your strategy, mission, and vision, the next step is to create a brand that encompasses all of these attributes. More than just a nice logo, the brand should represent and become the overall identity of the company. I suggest this because so often people start with a name and a logo, when they should first complete the steps to develop their mission, vision, and strategy, and then create the brand. In addition, people think brand is just a logo. One guy at a food show told me it is all about cosmetics. But of course it's much deeper than that."

LESSON FIVE: CAPITAL AND CASH FLOWS

After much preparation and research, the time finally comes to launch your company. Most companies require capital to get going. Money required for facilities, equipment, tools, raw materials, systems, expert help, and just to live on are often required to start a business. In fact, many entrepreneurs have to work another job or two while starting a venture on the side so they can maintain an income.

Getting the necessary capital to start your company is usually done through loans, venture capital (money from equity investors who require ownership in the company), personal money, or "friendly money" (money given or loaned on generous terms by family and friends).

While there are pros and cons to each, there are some basic questions to ask in order to determine the best source of obtaining capital. For instance, how much of the company and its control are you willing to give up? How fast do you need or want to grow? How big do you want to become? How risk-averse are you? How much money can you afford to lose? What are your long-term goals for the company? Can your projected cash flows sustain debt and, if so, how much? What is the minimum amount of capital you need? While most of the answers to these questions will be based on the nature of your industry; your company's mission, vision, and strategy; and your financial projections, the rest of the answers will come from personal preference.

Some entrepreneurs prefer to avoid debt altogether. Others avoid capital from equity investors who usually gobble up a lion's share of the company ownership and its control. Some entrepreneurs like to grow slowly, investing only their own money in the company. Some want to keep their business small and family owned, while others have an appetite for mammoth undertakings, requiring partners and huge sums of capital.

Basically, there is no one right way to obtain capital. However, while thinking through the various options for acquiring capital and how much you should acquire to start your business, here are some words of wisdom from multimillionaire entrepreneurs. One said to me, "Control is everything. So we weren't willing to give up equity. We didn't have any money. [My partner] borrowed a few dollars to live on, and we got vegetables from his brother's garden."

Another entrepreneur told me, "We had the philosophy of not investing anything we couldn't or weren't willing to afford to lose."

Mr. Huntsman said, "I started a company with my brother years ago in the record album industry. The money from that business helped me fund the chemical business. But I started the record business by going around to four banks trying to get money. I ended up getting a thousand dollars from each bank. That was a lot of money for me to borrow at that time. Pretty soon we made good money. But one time we needed additional money to produce records, because the stores we sold to wouldn't pay us for our records until after Christmas. So I contacted my four original banks and got a six-hundred-thousand-dollar loan with nothing on it. They trusted me. Start small and then protect what you have. Remember, every penny of borrowed money is more sacred than anything else you own. You must repay it. If you do, you soon get an open line of credit, and that's worth more than being a millionaire. You don't own it, but you can get it. Most people want short-cuts to get rich quick. But it's integrity and repaying everything you borrow ahead of time."

Another entrepreneur from a high-tech industry said, "We got a hundred and fifty thousand dollars for forty-nine percent of our stock." He and his partner's company grew to be worth many millions. However, he said that originally one particular venture capitalist wanted 60 percent of the stock, but he wouldn't consider that offer. He told me, "Control is everything. If you don't have control and the guy with the control wants to close you down one day, then that's what happens."

Another entrepreneur told me his story: "I had three thousand five hundred dollars to put into the company. That was all we had. Fourteen years later, we now have four thousand employees. I never had envisioned that this is what the company would become. This is a magnificent accident. But we had a serious passion for what we thought we could do. During the first four years of the company, we put everything we had into it. We mortgaged our home and two cars. I was taking thirty thousand dollars a year in salary for the first four years, because everything went back into the company. By the fifth year, I started taking home a decent salary. I tried to get loans, but banks wouldn't even call me back."

With Baker Mills, I didn't want to give up ownership outside the family, nor did I want to take out loans. However, we later had to do both in minor amounts. This course of action forced us to grow slowly, since our growth would be based on investing the very little personal money we had while reinvesting the profits we earned right back into the company. This model fit our mission and vision for the company, and we were happy with it. It also forced us to make wise, limited purchase decisions—a blessing in disguise.

Once you have capital to start your company, remember that from here on, cash flow is most important. "Watch your cash flows and profits .... Remember cash is king," a millionaire entrepreneur told me.

When I asked another for his advice on cash flow, he said, "Stay out of debt. As soon as entrepreneurs make some money they immediately go spend it on a new Mercedes and home.

However, I drive a Mercedes, but I can afford it. You must stay out of debt, the same way you run a household."

One entrepreneur told me that failed startups are often due to "trying to grow too fast. You must be careful with your resources and not overspend."

Another said, "Business owners begin buying oak furniture and expensive suits and they fail."

Remember, growing too quickly, spending money on unessential items, purchasing and storing excess inventory, and escalating accounts receivables kill cash flows. Keep costs down. Don't extend faster than you can afford from a projected cash flow perspective. Too many companies that grow too fast go out of business because they don't have sufficient cash left over to pay their bills. These companies tie up their money on filling orders and then wait for customers to pay them while vendor invoices and bills are overdue. These startups get into a cash bind. And when they find they can't borrow any more money, they go out of business.

When you experience early wins and increased customer demand, you will be tempted to grow too quickly. However, you must be disciplined and wise about your growth rate. Sometimes initial customer demands are simply a bubble that will soon dissipate. You don't want to build a big company based on a bubble of business and then be stuck with huge factories, warehouses, and capital equipment after the demand peaks and then slows or the economy breaks. Watch your projected cash flows—that is the key to longevity.

Simply said, you must exercise patience and self-control. Successful entrepreneurs are not complacent; they expand and develop their organizations at an appropriate rate and in a judicious manner. They realize that cash is king and retain in reserves the appropriate levels of cash to meet operational expenses, unforeseen costs, and economic variability, rather than waste cash on rushed growth, luxury items, and personal bank accounts.

My brother Joel adds, "Make sure you have enough money to get you through your worst-case scenario, and if you don't have enough money, then don't start the business—or think twice about starting it. We hear about the winners but not the countless losers who had no financial plans for their worst-case scenarios. Unless you're willing to go through many years of the frustrating pains of bootstrapping a resourceless business, then don't proceed."

LESSON SIX: ROOM AT THE TOP

As you launch your business, recognize that there is plenty of room for you to succeed even in the midst of formidable competition. One self-made millionaire entrepreneur told me, "There is always room at the top. You just tell everyone to slide over."

How do you accomplish this? Without taking your eye off product quality and performing the business fundamentals well—such as strategy, marketing, operations, and tight financial management—you have to be superior to your competition in at least one simple way. It is *dependability*. It's actually quite astonishing. However, because your competition will not be as effective at this as you can be, they leave the door open for you to capture much of their market share. This characteristic requires no capital, no formal training, no MBA. If you can be dependable, you will defeat much of your competition.

When starting Baker Mills I was often frustrated by the

number of suppliers and vendors who routinely failed to deliver on promises. It got to be so commonplace that we literally had to manage our vendors. They were making too many mistakes, some of which were quite costly. In response, we realized we had to assume control over our own destiny rather than leave it in the hands of suppliers and vendors. So we developed a company motto that we have operated by for more than a decade:

Everyone does everything wrong and no one ever gets back to you!

This motto put the burden back on our own shoulders to follow up with vendors to make sure they would deliver on time and perform the way we needed them to. Because we had no margin for error in the beginning, we couldn't afford vendors making mistakes. Nevertheless, it happened, and it became difficult to find vendors who would perform at consistently high levels. We went through many vendors while trying to find outstanding companies to do business with. During this process we always had one or two backup suppliers and vendors on deck to help us when our primary vendors dropped the ball.

Several times the vendors who manufactured our products added erroneous ingredients, like the wrong type of whole wheat flour, or they omitted ingredients, such as baking powder. At other times the packaging was unacceptable; the inside bag was sealed wrong or not sealed at all. In one instance, flour was somehow spilled all over the insides of the boxes. Unfortunately some of these flawed batches made it to the grocery stores and ultimately to the consumer before we identified the error. These mistakes led to lost customers and expensive recalls for our manufacturers.

On many occasions I have not been able to get sales representatives from potential vendors and manufacturers to call me back when I needed their services. I honestly couldn't get anybody to take my business. When I was first setting up Baker Mills, potential food suppliers, printers, and box manufacturers would not return my phone calls so I could purchase their products. When I finally did get a box printing company, they printed the wrong color on our packaging. I was dismayed.

One time one of our manufacturer imposed a price increase. They communicated the price increase to our distributors, who passed it on to the grocery stores. However, after the price increase went through and the product pricing was marked up in the stores, the manufacturer changed their mind and rescinded the price increase. Unfortunately the distributors didn't notify the grocery stores that the price increase had been retracted. For nearly a year the stores were charging too much and we were losing customers. And while the distributors and grocery stores were making additional revenue on the price increase, we were still operating under old prices.

We frequently placed orders with our manufacturers specifying that a particular grocery store chain needed so many pallets of product by a certain date. We were later caught off guard when the grocery stores called us wondering where their orders were. Then, of course, we contacted our manufacturers to find that they forgot about the order or for whatever reason never produced it. We quickly learned to follow up on orders we placed to avoid these problems in the future.

The point of lesson six is that while mistakes do and will happen, most mistakes can be avoided if businesses are simply dependable. Imagine how great it would be if you called a company to place an order, and you received exactly what you ordered on time? What if a subcontractor called you back and then showed up at your business when he said he would? As a new company you must operate dependably, since far too many businesses don't. You cannot drop the ball. In addition, you must manage your vendors to ensure that they don't drop the ball either. If you operate this way, you will have an edge on your competition, and they will be forced to slide over for you, as customers quickly learn they can always count on you.

LESSON SEVEN: SALES AND PUBLIC RELATIONS

Most successful entrepreneurs I know have the innate ability to sell. They are courageous, charismatic, and possess outstanding interpersonal skills. Customers often purchase their products just because they like the entrepreneur. Sales, I have learned, are often a function of good, honest relationships. One entrepreneur said to me, "Security is not an issue for an entrepreneur. My security is not wrapped up in [my business], but in my ability to sell. You have to know how to sell, or you'll never be an entrepreneur. Especially in the beginning, you've got to be able to sell."

Joel, my Dad, and I have no fear in selling. For many, however, selling is a loathsome task. Because of this strong dislike and even resistance to selling, many entrepreneurs incorporate a reactive rather than proactive approach to generating business. They expect customers to call them to do business, rather than going out and getting it themselves. As a result, more often than not, their businesses grow very slowly or not at all. To be a successful entrepreneur, you must sell or you must have a sales plan that proactively creates business. In addition, as you start your business, your sales plan must be front-end-loaded, requiring relentless tenacity in the first months. Operate under the assumption that sales won't come to you when you open your doors, but that you must aggressively go after them. One great entrepreneur told me, "Be bold in the advertising and the marketing of a product."

When Joel, my Dad, and I attended a huge food show in San Francisco, we proactively sold Kodiak Cakes at our booth, often walking out into the aisle and telling people about our product. We cheerfully and enthusiastically approached people and said things like, "You have got to sample our Kodiak Cakes—they will change your life!" People would come over, taste the product, and love it. We gave them a fun experience. However, at hundreds of other booths the vendors just sat on chairs waiting for people to approach them and ask about the food product they were selling. These vendors looked bored and even miserable. I saw only a small handful of companies really selling their products. But this is how you must tackle sales. You have to smile, show some energy, and get after it. You need to be likeable. People want to be sold.

If you can't be enthusiastic and happy in promoting your product, you must hire someone who will. Unfortunately, since most sales representatives won't care personally about your product the way you do, you need to hire the right people who love your product and will sell it. We've hired food brokers, for example, who gave our brand such little attention that we ended up letting them go and doing most of the sales promotion ourselves.

Beyond direct person-to-person selling, promoting a product requires capital. When we set up Kodiak Cakes, we didn't have the budget to produce and air commercials on television like so many other food companies do. We had to show ingenuity. But part of the fun of business is that you will always have a limited budget to work with, requiring you to strategize and figure out how you can make a profit.

So what other methods are there to inexpensively and effectively promote your product? The answer lies in public relations. This area encompasses free advertisement through the media as press releases and stories are developed and communicated to the public. Joel moved forward with this plan and boldly contacted news and radio stations, newspapers, and magazines to see if they would write stories on Baker Mills and Kodiak Cakes. It proved to be most effective and saved us thousands of dollars in marketing costs.

The other thing we learned while promoting our products through public relations is that new startups must provide customers with an incentive to switch over to their brand. Most often new companies have to buy their way into the market by offering a lower price or some kind of deal. This initially lowers profitability, but it is often the only way to get customers to buy your product. Once they do, their experience should bring them back and generate the desired word-of-mouth marketing.

LESSON EIGHT: LEVERAGE YOUR STRENGTHS

Since the functions of starting and operating a company are so demanding and diverse, it's difficult for an entrepreneur to be extremely proficient in all areas. In fact, most entrepreneurs are great, even world-class, at one or two, but not so talented at others. When my brother Joel was exploring the option of self-manufacturing Kodiak Cakes, I told him, "Joel, you are a world-class marketer, but probably not a world-class production manager." He laughed and knew his time would be better spent leveraging his strengths while other experts performed the manufacturing functions for us.

This is true for most of us. You may be world-class at sales, but you may be somewhat inadequate at accounting, graphic art, computer networking, or even administration, which can all be performed by others. Objectively distinguishing your strengths from your weaknesses and getting the needed assistance requires self-awareness and perhaps a little humility, but it creates the potential for greater success in return. I knew an entrepreneur who was an exceptionally gifted marketer and strategist but a less effective operating officer. Consequently he hired someone else to fill this role as president of his own company.

One entrepreneur told me, "The number one thing is you must be willing to admit you don't know how to do certain things. For example, I hate accounting and I'm not good at it. But I'm not embarrassed about it. I just got someone who is good at it."

Another said, "An entrepreneur must get the right people around him, with complementary skills, who know something about finance or technology."

A third told me: "I make sure I work with really good people. You have to be supported by very competent people all around you. Business is team based; you just can't do it alone. For example, a business is started by an inventor, it grows by the marketing guy, it's manufactured by the production guy, and it's sold by the sales guy. Different people come in and help the company throughout the various stages of the life cycle of the company. Different people come in as different needs arise." Leveraging your strengths will build your company as fast as any other way.

LESSON NINE: BUSINESS OWNER REALITY

While you are trying to leverage your strengths, you may have to initially perform many business functions that you know you aren't good at. This doesn't mean you can't leverage your strengths; it just means you will be stretched and tasked to do things outside your area of expertise for a time. While most entrepreneurs choose to go into a business they are passionate about, they are often significantly restricted from spending their time in the areas they love. For instance, if you want to open a bakery because you love to bake, you will most likely not be able to bake as much as you want to, at least initially. This is because the reality of owning a business typically requires you to market and sell, maintain the books, manage employees, and perform many other responsibilities.

For many, this becomes discouraging as they devote their time to things they aren't good at and don't enjoy. In fact, it can also cripple the business, because while you could be leveraging your strengths to further the company, you are tied to a desk answering phones, taking orders, invoicing customers, and paying bills. It can be frustrating, but you should expect it to happen. The purpose of this lesson is to prepare you to comprehend the reality of what you are about to face as an entrepreneur.

In fact, this is often why most entrepreneurs feel overworked. They don't have the capital to sustain their livelihood while starting a business, so they have to work two jobs for a while. They also can't hire the experts they need to help start the business, so they have to perform all the functions themselves. Many of these functions are mundane, office-related tasks that drag on for many hours a week. As a result, overworked entrepreneurs feel stressed.

In addition, performing so many functions without the help of others makes entrepreneurship feel like a lonely occupation in the starting months—or even years. Because you can't afford to hire other people and have to do it yourself, you work alone a lot of the time. This can be extremely discouraging and can even negatively impact your excitement and motivation to keep getting up early each day to go to work on your company. Many entrepreneurs are tempted to quit and go back to an employer during these stages. But this is often the reality of the career at its outset. You must hang on until things get better. The price is worth it in the end.

On the flip side, however, entrepreneurs who start their companies with plenty of capital can leverage themselves to fulfill the functions they are best at. They are excited about the focused work they are engaged in. They have people around them to talk to and bounce ideas off. However, this luxury of having lots of capital can cause entrepreneurs to become complacent, since they don't have to fight for success like the lone entrepreneur with little capital. In the end, this latter type of entrepreneur is like a lonely old oak tree that weathered the storms and stood strong, though not without its share of battle wounds and broken branches.

LESSON TEN: SUCCESS AND PHILANTHROPY

Understanding and applying the previous nine lessons will greatly enhance your chances for success as an entrepreneur. However, as one entrepreneur told me, "When you become successful, don't get an ego and let it go to your head." In addition, share your success with those around you. Seek ways to reinvest it in your employees, those who helped you become successful, and your community. No entrepreneur can do it alone. Successful entrepreneurs recognize their dependency on others.

Baker Mills' success is attributed to many people who participated in various ways to make Kodiak Cakes the world's best flapjack and waffle mix. Suppliers, vendors, employees, friends, family, customers, and so many others profoundly contributed. In fact, there would be no Baker Mills without them, especially my brother Joel, who worked tirelessly for so many years making the company a success.

The goal of being successful is not to solely enjoy your own prosperity, but to share it. Likewise, I believe the American dream was never intended to bring a better life to just the one person who pursues and achieves it, but to family, friends, loved ones, future generations, and unknown others, through your generous contributions and philanthropies.

When commenting on why others are unsuccessful in starting their own companies, one entrepreneur told me, "They don't give away a piece of the rock to those around them who helped them build the company. We were a Subchapter S corporation, which means we could have only thirty-five shareholders. Every one of those thirty-five became millionaires. I've got to feel pretty good about that." He went on to say, "We give away a lot of what we earn. I've given away fifty million dollars. It's the 'abundant mentality.' If you cast your bread upon the waters, it will come back to you. It's a natural law."

And so it is with your success. Your humble and often unnoticed philanthropy will cycle into even further success and greater dividends for you. People will esteem you all the more for your sincere generosity and concern for the well-being of others.